STAY UP TO DATE ON FUTURE BOOKS & DEALS

SCAN THE QR CODE BELOW TO BE INCLUDED IN FUTURE BOOKS, SPECIALS DEALS, DISCOUNTS, AND FREE GIVEAWAYS! SIMPLY SCAN BELOW WITH YOUR CELL PHONE AND CLICK ON ENTER EMAIL ADDRESS TAB AND WE WILL DO THE REST. THAT'S IT!

IDEAS AND NOTES

Name: _____

THIS BOOK BELONGS TO:

CONTACT INFORMATION	
NAME:	
ADDRESS:	
PHONE:	

START / END DATES

___ / ___ / ___   TO   ___ / ___ / ___

RV LOGBOOK

CAMPGROUND:		DATE:
LOCATION:		
TRAVEL TO CAMPGROUND: MILES:	TIME:	COAST:
WEATHER:	TEMPERATURE:	

CAMPGROUND INFORMATION

NAME:		AMENITIES	
ADDRESS:	□ SEWER	□ PULL THROUGH	□ BACK-IN
PHONE:	□ PAVED	□ PET FRIENDLY	□ LAUNDRY
SITE:	□ WATER	□ EASY ACCESS	□ ELECTRICITY
COAST:	□ 15 AMP	□ 30 AMP	□ 50 AMP
	□ SHADE	□ POOL	□ RESTROOMS
GPS:	□ STORE	□ PICNIC TABLE	□ FIRE RING
RATING: ☆ ☆ ☆ ☆ ☆ ☆ ☆ ☆ ☆	□ FIREWOOD	□ TV	□ WIFI
WATER PRESSURE ☆ ☆ ☆ ☆ ☆	□ SECURITY	□ ICE	□ CAFE

		ACTIVITIES	
CLEANLINESS ☆ ☆ ☆ ☆ ☆	□ FISHING	□ SHUFFLEBOARD	□ BOAT
LOCATION ☆ ☆ ☆ ☆ ☆	□ LAKE	□ PICKLEBALL	□ GOLF
SITE SIZE ☆ ☆ ☆ ☆ ☆	□ BIKE	□ CANOEING	□ FITNESS
NOISE ☆ ☆ ☆ ☆ ☆	□ HIKING	□ HOT TUB	□ RIVER
RESTROOMS ☆ ☆ ☆ ☆ ☆			

CAMPED WITH		TO DO LIST
		□
		□
		□
PEOPLE MET		□
		□
		□
		□
		□
PLACES VISITED		□
		□
		□

DATE LOG BOOK STARTED:	DATE LOG BOOK COMPLETED:

RV CAMPGROUND LOG

CAMPGROUND:			DATE:
LOCATION:			RESERVATION NO.:
CONTACT:			SITE NO.:
WEBSITE:		NEARBY TOWN/CITY:	
DAILY RATE:	TOTAL:	ELECTRIC: ☐ 30 AMP ☐ 50 AMP	METER READING:
DISCOUNT USED:	PET FRIENDLY: ☐ YES ☐ NO	DUMP STATION: ☐ SITE ☐ COMMUNITY ☐ HONEY DIPPER	
WIFI: ☐ EXCELLENT ☐ GOOD ☐ BAD ☐ VERY BAD		WATER: ☐ EXCELLENT ☐ GOOD ☐ BAD ☐ VERY BAD	
NOTES:		NOTES:	

FAVORITE SITES FOR NEXT VISIT:

POOL	SHOWERS	BIKE RENTALS	FISHING
HOT TUB	GROCERIES	BOAT RENTALS	RESTROOMS
CAMP STORE	LAUNDRY	NATURE TRAILS	HIKING
FITNESS ROOM	FIREWOOD	LAKE	ENTERTAINMENT

OTHER AMENITIES:

OTHER ACTIVITIES:

MOST MEMORABLE EVENT:

MOST FUN THINGS:

CAMPGROUND SCENERY:

WILDLIFE:

NOTES:

RV CAMPGROUND LOG

CAMPGROUND:	DATE:
LOCATION:	RESERVATION NO.:
CONTACT:	SITE NO.:

WEBSITE:		NEARBY TOWN/CITY:	
DAILY RATE:	TOTAL:	ELECTRIC: ☐ 30 AMP ☐ 50 AMP	METER READING:
DISCOUNT USED:	PET FRIENDLY: ☐ YES ☐ NO	DUMP STATION: ☐ SITE ☐ COMMUNITY ☐ HONEY DIPPER	

WIFI: ☐ EXCELLENT ☐ GOOD ☐ BAD ☐ VERY BAD	WATER: ☐ EXCELLENT ☐ GOOD ☐ BAD ☐ VERY BAD
NOTES:	NOTES:

FAVORITE SITES FOR NEXT VISIT:

POOL	SHOWERS	BIKE RENTALS	FISHING
HOT TUB	GROCERIES	BOAT RENTALS	RESTROOMS
CAMP STORE	LAUNDRY	NATURE TRAILS	HIKING
FITNESS ROOM	FIREWOOD	LAKE	ENTERTAINMENT

OTHER AMENITIES:

OTHER ACTIVITIES:

MOST MEMORABLE EVENT:

MOST FUN THINGS:

CAMPGROUND SCENERY:

WILDLIFE:

NOTES:

RV CAMPGROUND LOGBOOK

MANAGEMENT / BOOKING / CANCELLATION NOTES:

MANEUVERING / PARKING: ☐ TIGHT ROADS / TURNS   ☐ LOW-HANGING TREES   ☐ BAD ROAD CONDITIONS

OTHER PARKING NOTES:

SITE-SPECIFIC NOTES:	SITE NUMBER STAYED IN:

SITE HOOK UPS: ☐ FHU   ☐ W/E ONLY   ☐ 50 AMP   ☐ 30 AMP   ☐ DRY CAMPING

RV PAD: ☐ LEVEL ☐ UNLEVEL   ☐ CONCRETE   ☐ ROCK   ☐ GRASS   ☐ DIRT   OTHER:

SITE SIZE: ☐ TIGHT   ☐ MODERATE   ☐ SPACIOUS   ☐ VERY LARGE

TREES / SHADE: ☐ FULL SUN   ☐ SOME SHADE   ☐ A LOT OF SHADE

FIRE RING / PIT: ☐ YES ☐ NO	FIRES ALLOWED: ☐ YES ☐ NO
PICNIC TABLE: ☐ YES ☐ NO	NICE VIEW: ☐ YES ☐ NO

CLOSE TO AMENITIES: ☐ YES   ☐ NO

NOISE:

WILDLIFE:

OTHER:

DRAWING OF SITE OR FAVORITE PHOTO:

RV CAMPGROUND LOGBOOK

MANAGEMENT / BOOKING / CANCELLATION NOTES:

MANEUVERING / PARKING: ☐ TIGHT ROADS / TURNS   ☐ LOW-HANGING TREES   ☐ BAD ROAD CONDITIONS

OTHER PARKING NOTES:

SITE-SPECIFIC NOTES: | SITE NUMBER STAYED IN:

SITE HOOK UPS: ☐ FHU   ☐ W/E ONLY   ☐ 50 AMP   ☐ 30 AMP   ☐ DRY CAMPING

RV PAD: ☐ LEVEL ☐ UNLEVEL   ☐ CONCRETE   ☐ ROCK   ☐ GRASS   ☐ DIRT   OTHER:

SITE SIZE: ☐ TIGHT   ☐ MODERATE   ☐ SPACIOUS   ☐ VERY LARGE

TREES / SHADE: ☐ FULL SUN   ☐ SOME SHADE   ☐ A LOT OF SHADE

FIRE RING / PIT: ☐ YES   ☐ NO   FIRES ALLOWED: ☐ YES   ☐ NO

PICNIC TABLE: ☐ YES   ☐ NO   NICE VIEW: ☐ YES   ☐ NO

CLOSE TO AMENITIES: ☐ YES   ☐ NO

NOISE:

WILDLIFE:

OTHER:

DRAWING OF SITE OR FAVORITE PHOTO:

RV CAMPGROUND LOGBOOK

LOCAL AREA NOTES				
WEATHER DURING STAY:	☐ VERY COLD	☐ COLD	☐ MODERATE	☐ WARM ☐ HOT
OTHER WEATHER NOTES:				
NEARBY SIGHTSEEING:				
NEARBY RESTAURANTS:				
NEARBY GROCERY STORE:	☐ 0-5 MIN.	☐ 5-10 MIN	☐ 10-20 MIN.	☐ 20-30 MIN. ☐ 30+ MIN.
OTHER GROCERY NOTES:				
NEARBY PLACES VISITED:				
VISIT / DO NEXT TIME:				

DESTINATION:	DATES:
TRAVELLED FROM:	TO
VIA	MILEAGE

PREFERRED ROUTES / ROUTES TO AVOID:

SITES ALONG THE WAY:

WEATHER:

CAMPGROUND (NAME, LOCATION, CONTACT, FEES, RESERVATION)

CAMPGROUND PROS AND CONS:

CAMPSITE NUMBER AND DESCRIPTION:

THINGS TO AVOID NEXT TIME:

TRAVELLING COMPANIONS:

THINGS TO REMEMBER FOR NEXT TIME:

RV CAMPGROUND LOGBOOK

LOCAL AREA NOTES				
WEATHER DURING STAY: ☐ VERY COLD	☐ COLD	☐ MODERATE	☐ WARM	☐ HOT
OTHER WEATHER NOTES:				
NEARBY SIGHTSEEING:				
NEARBY RESTAURANTS:				
NEARBY GROCERY STORE: ☐ 0-5 MIN.	☐ 5-10 MIN	☐ 10-20 MIN.	☐ 20-30 MIN.	☐ 30+ MIN.
OTHER GROCERY NOTES:				
NEARBY PLACES VISITED:				
VISIT / DO NEXT TIME:				

DESTINATION:	DATES:
TRAVELLED FROM:	TO
VIA	MILEAGE
PREFERRED ROUTES / ROUTES TO AVOID:	
SITES ALONG THE WAY:	
WEATHER:	
CAMPGROUND (NAME, LOCATION, CONTACT, FEES, RESERVATION)	
CAMPGROUND PROS AND CONS:	
CAMPSITE NUMBER AND DESCRIPTION:	
THINGS TO AVOID NEXT TIME:	
TRAVELLING COMPANIONS:	
THINGS TO REMEMBER FOR NEXT TIME:	

RV PHOTO GALLERY

LOCATION		LOCATION	
PHOTO		PHOTO	
DATE:		DATE:	

LOCATION		LOCATION	
PHOTO		PHOTO	
DATE:		DATE:	

LOCATION		LOCATION	
PHOTO		PHOTO	
DATE:		DATE:	

NOTES	

RV PHOTO GALLERY

LOCATION		LOCATION	
	PHOTO		PHOTO
DATE:		DATE:	

LOCATION		LOCATION	
	PHOTO		PHOTO
DATE:		DATE:	

LOCATION		LOCATION	
	PHOTO		PHOTO
DATE:		DATE:	

NOTES	

DAILY RV PLANNER

	DESTINATION	ACTIVITIES
DAY 1		
DAY 2		
DAY 3		
DAY 4		
DAY 5		
DAY 6		
DAY 7		

DAILY RV PLANNER

	DESTINATION	ACTIVITIES
DAY 1		
DAY 2		
DAY 3		
DAY 4		
DAY 5		
DAY 6		
DAY 7		

WEEKLY RV SCHEDULE

LOCATION	SUN	MON	TUE	WED	THU	FRI	SAT

REMINDERS	LIST
○	○
○	○
○	○
○	○
○	○
○	○
○	○
○	○
○	○
○	○
○	○
○	○

WEEKLY RV SCHEDULE

LOCATION	SUN	MON	TUE	WED	THU	FRI	SAT

REMINDERS	LIST
○	○
○	○
○	○
○	○
○	○
○	○
○	○
○	○
○	○
○	○
○	○
○	○

INDEX

RV LOGBOOK

CAMPGROUND:		DATE:
LOCATION:		
TRAVEL TO CAMPGROUND: MILES:	TIME:	COAST:
WEATHER:	TEMPERATURE:	

CAMPGROUND INFORMATION

NAME:

ADDRESS:

PHONE:

SITE:

COAST:

GPS:

RATING: ☆ ☆ ☆ ☆ ☆ ☆ ☆ ☆ ☆ ☆

WATER PRESSURE	☆ ☆ ☆ ☆ ☆
CLEANLINESS	☆ ☆ ☆ ☆ ☆
LOCATION	☆ ☆ ☆ ☆ ☆
SITE SIZE	☆ ☆ ☆ ☆ ☆
NOISE	☆ ☆ ☆ ☆ ☆
RESTROOMS	☆ ☆ ☆ ☆ ☆

AMENITIES

☐ SEWER	☐ PULL THROUGH	☐ BACK-IN
☐ PAVED	☐ PET FRIENDLY	☐ LAUNDRY
☐ WATER	☐ EASY ACCESS	☐ ELECTRICITY
☐ 15 AMP	☐ 30 AMP	☐ 50 AMP
☐ SHADE	☐ POOL	☐ RESTROOMS
☐ STORE	☐ PICNIC TABLE	☐ FIRE RING
☐ FIREWOOD	☐ TV	☐ WIFI
☐ SECURITY	☐ ICE	☐ CAFE

ACTIVITIES

☐ FISHING	☐ SHUFFLEBOARD	☐ BOAT
☐ LAKE	☐ PICKLEBALL	☐ GOLF
☐ BIKE	☐ CANOEING	☐ FITNESS
☐ HIKING	☐ HOT TUB	☐ RIVER

CAMPED WITH		TO DO LIST
		☐
		☐
		☐
PEOPLE MET		☐
		☐
		☐
		☐
		☐
PLACES VISITED		☐
		☐
		☐

DATE LOG BOOK STARTED:	DATE LOG BOOK COMPLETED:

RV CAMPGROUND LOG

CAMPGROUND:			DATE:
LOCATION:			RESERVATION NO.:
CONTACT:			SITE NO.:
WEBSITE:		NEARBY TOWN/CITY:	
DAILY RATE:	TOTAL:	ELECTRIC: ☐ 30 AMP ☐ 50 AMP	METER READING:
DISCOUNT USED:	PET FRIENDLY: ☐ YES ☐ NO	DUMP STATION: ☐ SITE ☐ COMMUNITY ☐ HONEY DIPPER	
WIFI: ☐ EXCELLENT ☐ GOOD ☐ BAD ☐ VERY BAD		WATER: ☐ EXCELLENT ☐ GOOD ☐ BAD ☐ VERY BAD	
NOTES:		NOTES:	

FAVORITE SITES FOR NEXT VISIT:

POOL	SHOWERS	BIKE RENTALS	FISHING
HOT TUB	GROCERIES	BOAT RENTALS	RESTROOMS
CAMP STORE	LAUNDRY	NATURE TRAILS	HIKING
FITNESS ROOM	FIREWOOD	LAKE	ENTERTAINMENT

OTHER AMENITIES:

OTHER ACTIVITIES:

MOST MEMORABLE EVENT:

MOST FUN THINGS:

CAMPGROUND SCENERY:

WILDLIFE:

NOTES:

RV CAMPGROUND LOG

CAMPGROUND:		DATE:
LOCATION:		RESERVATION NO.:
CONTACT:		SITE NO.:

WEBSITE:		NEARBY TOWN/CITY:	
DAILY RATE:	TOTAL:	ELECTRIC: ☐ 30 AMP ☐ 50 AMP	METER READING:
DISCOUNT USED:	PET FRIENDLY: ☐ YES ☐ NO	DUMP STATION: ☐ SITE ☐ COMMUNITY ☐ HONEY DIPPER	
WIFI: ☐ EXCELLENT ☐ GOOD ☐ BAD ☐ VERY BAD		WATER: ☐ EXCELLENT ☐ GOOD ☐ BAD ☐ VERY BAD	
NOTES:		NOTES:	

FAVORITE SITES FOR NEXT VISIT:

POOL	SHOWERS	BIKE RENTALS	FISHING
HOT TUB	GROCERIES	BOAT RENTALS	RESTROOMS
CAMP STORE	LAUNDRY	NATURE TRAILS	HIKING
FITNESS ROOM	FIREWOOD	LAKE	ENTERTAINMENT

OTHER AMENITIES:

OTHER ACTIVITIES:

MOST MEMORABLE EVENT:

MOST FUN THINGS:

CAMPGROUND SCENERY:

WILDLIFE:

NOTES:

RV CAMPGROUND LOGBOOK

MANAGEMENT / BOOKING / CANCELLATION NOTES:

MANEUVERING / PARKING: ☐ TIGHT ROADS / TURNS   ☐ LOW-HANGING TREES   ☐ BAD ROAD CONDITIONS

OTHER PARKING NOTES:

SITE-SPECIFIC NOTES: SITE NUMBER STAYED IN:

SITE HOOK UPS: ☐ FHU   ☐ W/E ONLY   ☐ 50 AMP   ☐ 30 AMP   ☐ DRY CAMPING

RV PAD: ☐ LEVEL ☐ UNLEVEL   ☐ CONCRETE   ☐ ROCK   ☐ GRASS   ☐ DIRT   OTHER:

SITE SIZE: ☐ TIGHT   ☐ MODERATE   ☐ SPACIOUS   ☐ VERY LARGE

TREES / SHADE: ☐ FULL SUN   ☐ SOME SHADE   ☐ A LOT OF SHADE

FIRE RING / PIT: ☐ YES   ☐ NO   FIRES ALLOWED: ☐ YES   ☐ NO

PICNIC TABLE: ☐ YES   ☐ NO   NICE VIEW: ☐ YES   ☐ NO

CLOSE TO AMENITIES: ☐ YES   ☐ NO

NOISE:

WILDLIFE:

OTHER:

DRAWING OF SITE OR FAVORITE PHOTO:

RV CAMPGROUND LOGBOOK

MANAGEMENT / BOOKING / CANCELLATION NOTES:

MANEUVERING / PARKING: ☐ TIGHT ROADS / TURNS   ☐ LOW-HANGING TREES   ☐ BAD ROAD CONDITIONS

OTHER PARKING NOTES:

SITE-SPECIFIC NOTES: | SITE NUMBER STAYED IN:

SITE HOOK UPS: ☐ FHU   ☐ W/E ONLY   ☐ 50 AMP   ☐ 30 AMP   ☐ DRY CAMPING

RV PAD: ☐ LEVEL ☐ UNLEVEL   ☐ CONCRETE   ☐ ROCK   ☐ GRASS   ☐ DIRT   OTHER:

SITE SIZE: ☐ TIGHT   ☐ MODERATE   ☐ SPACIOUS   ☐ VERY LARGE

TREES / SHADE: ☐ FULL SUN   ☐ SOME SHADE   ☐ A LOT OF SHADE

FIRE RING / PIT: ☐ YES   ☐ NO   FIRES ALLOWED: ☐ YES   ☐ NO

PICNIC TABLE: ☐ YES   ☐ NO   NICE VIEW: ☐ YES   ☐ NO

CLOSE TO AMENITIES: ☐ YES   ☐ NO

NOISE:

WILDLIFE:

OTHER:

DRAWING OF SITE OR FAVORITE PHOTO:

RV CAMPGROUND LOGBOOK

LOCAL AREA NOTES				
WEATHER DURING STAY:	☐ VERY COLD	☐ COLD	☐ MODERATE	☐ WARM ☐ HOT
OTHER WEATHER NOTES:				
NEARBY SIGHTSEEING:				
NEARBY RESTAURANTS:				
NEARBY GROCERY STORE:	☐ 0-5 MIN.	☐ 5-10 MIN	☐ 10-20 MIN.	☐ 20-30 MIN. ☐ 30+ MIN.
OTHER GROCERY NOTES:				
NEARBY PLACES VISITED:				
VISIT / DO NEXT TIME:				

DESTINATION:	DATES:
TRAVELLED FROM:	TO
VIA	MILEAGE
PREFERRED ROUTES / ROUTES TO AVOID:	
SITES ALONG THE WAY:	
WEATHER:	
CAMPGROUND (NAME, LOCATION, CONTACT, FEES, RESERVATION)	
CAMPGROUND PROS AND CONS:	
CAMPSITE NUMBER AND DESCRIPTION:	
THINGS TO AVOID NEXT TIME:	
TRAVELLING COMPANIONS:	
THINGS TO REMEMBER FOR NEXT TIME:	

RV CAMPGROUND LOGBOOK

LOCAL AREA NOTES				
WEATHER DURING STAY: ☐ VERY COLD	☐ COLD	☐ MODERATE	☐ WARM	☐ HOT
OTHER WEATHER NOTES:				
NEARBY SIGHTSEEING:				
NEARBY RESTAURANTS:				
NEARBY GROCERY STORE: ☐ 0-5 MIN.	☐ 5-10 MIN	☐ 10-20 MIN.	☐ 20-30 MIN.	☐ 30+ MIN.
OTHER GROCERY NOTES:				
NEARBY PLACES VISITED:				
VISIT / DO NEXT TIME:				

DESTINATION:	DATES:
TRAVELLED FROM:	TO
VIA	MILEAGE
PREFERRED ROUTES / ROUTES TO AVOID:	
SITES ALONG THE WAY:	
WEATHER:	
CAMPGROUND (NAME, LOCATION, CONTACT, FEES, RESERVATION)	
CAMPGROUND PROS AND CONS:	
CAMPSITE NUMBER AND DESCRIPTION:	
THINGS TO AVOID NEXT TIME:	
TRAVELLING COMPANIONS:	
THINGS TO REMEMBER FOR NEXT TIME:	

RV PHOTO GALLERY

LOCATION	LOCATION
PHOTO	PHOTO
DATE:	DATE:

LOCATION	LOCATION
PHOTO	PHOTO
DATE:	DATE:

LOCATION	LOCATION
PHOTO	PHOTO
DATE:	DATE:

NOTES

RV PHOTO GALLERY

LOCATION		LOCATION	
PHOTO		PHOTO	
DATE:		DATE:	

LOCATION		LOCATION	
PHOTO		PHOTO	
DATE:		DATE:	

LOCATION		LOCATION	
PHOTO		PHOTO	
DATE:		DATE:	

NOTES

DAILY RV PLANNER

	DESTINATION	ACTIVITIES
DAY 1		
DAY 2		
DAY 3		
DAY 4		
DAY 5		
DAY 6		
DAY 7		

DAILY RV PLANNER

	DESTINATION	ACTIVITIES
DAY 1		
DAY 2		
DAY 3		
DAY 4		
DAY 5		
DAY 6		
DAY 7		

WEEKLY RV SCHEDULE

LOCATION	SUN	MON	TUE	WED	THU	FRI	SAT

REMINDERS	LIST
○	○
○	○
○	○
○	○
○	○
○	○
○	○
○	○
○	○
○	○
○	○
○	○

WEEKLY RV SCHEDULE

LOCATION	SUN	MON	TUE	WED	THU	FRI	SAT

REMINDERS	LIST
○	○
○	○
○	○
○	○
○	○
○	○
○	○
○	○
○	○
○	○
○	○
○	○

INDEX

RV LOGBOOK

CAMPGROUND:		DATE:
LOCATION:		
TRAVEL TO CAMPGROUND: MILES:	TIME:	COAST:
WEATHER:	TEMPERATURE:	

CAMPGROUND INFORMATION

NAME:	AMENITIES		
ADDRESS:	☐ SEWER	☐ PULL THROUGH	☐ BACK-IN
PHONE:	☐ PAVED	☐ PET FRIENDLY	☐ LAUNDRY
SITE:	☐ WATER	☐ EASY ACCESS	☐ ELECTRICITY
COAST:	☐ 15 AMP	☐ 30 AMP	☐ 50 AMP
	☐ SHADE	☐ POOL	☐ RESTROOMS
GPS:	☐ STORE	☐ PICNIC TABLE	☐ FIRE RING
RATING:☆ ☆ ☆ ☆ ☆ ☆ ☆ ☆ ☆ ☆	☐ FIREWOOD	☐ TV	☐ WIFI

		AMENITIES		
WATER PRESSURE	☆ ☆ ☆ ☆ ☆	☐ SECURITY	☐ ICE	☐ CAFE
CLEANLINESS	☆ ☆ ☆ ☆ ☆	ACTIVITIES		
LOCATION	☆ ☆ ☆ ☆ ☆	☐ FISHING	☐ SHUFFLEBOARD	☐ BOAT
SITE SIZE	☆ ☆ ☆ ☆ ☆	☐ LAKE	☐ PICKLEBALL	☐ GOLF
NOISE	☆ ☆ ☆ ☆ ☆	☐ BIKE	☐ CANOEING	☐ FITNESS
RESTROOMS	☆ ☆ ☆ ☆ ☆	☐ HIKING	☐ HOT TUB	☐ RIVER

CAMPED WITH		TO DO LIST	
		☐	
		☐	
		☐	
PEOPLE MET		☐	
		☐	
		☐	
		☐	
		☐	
PLACES VISITED		☐	
		☐	
		☐	

DATE LOG BOOK STARTED:	DATE LOG BOOK COMPLETED:

RV CAMPGROUND LOG

CAMPGROUND:			DATE:
LOCATION:			RESERVATION NO.:
CONTACT:			SITE NO.:

WEBSITE:		NEARBY TOWN/CITY:	
DAILY RATE:	TOTAL:	ELECTRIC: ☐ 30 AMP ☐ 50 AMP	METER READING:
DISCOUNT USED:	PET FRIENDLY: ☐ YES ☐ NO	DUMP STATION: ☐ SITE ☐ COMMUNITY ☐ HONEY DIPPER	

WIFI: ☐ EXCELLENT ☐ GOOD ☐ BAD ☐ VERY BAD	WATER: ☐ EXCELLENT ☐ GOOD ☐ BAD ☐ VERY BAD
NOTES:	NOTES:

FAVORITE SITES FOR NEXT VISIT:

POOL	SHOWERS	BIKE RENTALS	FISHING
HOT TUB	GROCERIES	BOAT RENTALS	RESTROOMS
CAMP STORE	LAUNDRY	NATURE TRAILS	HIKING
FITNESS ROOM	FIREWOOD	LAKE	ENTERTAINMENT

OTHER AMENITIES:

OTHER ACTIVITIES:

MOST MEMORABLE EVENT:

MOST FUN THINGS:

CAMPGROUND SCENERY:

WILDLIFE:

NOTES:

RV CAMPGROUND LOG

CAMPGROUND:		DATE:
LOCATION:		RESERVATION NO.:
CONTACT:		SITE NO.:

| WEBSITE: | NEARBY TOWN/CITY: |

| DAILY RATE: | TOTAL: | ELECTRIC:
☐ 30 AMP   ☐ 50 AMP | METER READING: |

| DISCOUNT USED: | PET FRIENDLY:
☐ YES   ☐ NO | DUMP STATION:
☐ SITE   ☐ COMMUNITY   ☐ HONEY DIPPER |

| WIFI:
☐ EXCELLENT   ☐ GOOD   ☐ BAD   ☐ VERY BAD | WATER:
☐ EXCELLENT   ☐ GOOD   ☐ BAD   ☐ VERY BAD |
| NOTES: | NOTES: |

FAVORITE SITES FOR NEXT VISIT:

POOL	SHOWERS	BIKE RENTALS	FISHING
HOT TUB	GROCERIES	BOAT RENTALS	RESTROOMS
CAMP STORE	LAUNDRY	NATURE TRAILS	HIKING
FITNESS ROOM	FIREWOOD	LAKE	ENTERTAINMENT

OTHER AMENITIES:

OTHER ACTIVITIES:

MOST MEMORABLE EVENT:

MOST FUN THINGS:

CAMPGROUND SCENERY:

WILDLIFE:

NOTES:

RV CAMPGROUND LOGBOOK

MANAGEMENT / BOOKING / CANCELLATION NOTES:

MANEUVERING / PARKING: ☐ TIGHT ROADS / TURNS ☐ LOW-HANGING TREES ☐ BAD ROAD CONDITIONS
OTHER PARKING NOTES:

SITE-SPECIFIC NOTES:	SITE NUMBER STAYED IN:
SITE HOOK UPS: ☐ FHU ☐ W/E ONLY ☐ 50 AMP ☐ 30 AMP ☐ DRY CAMPING	
RV PAD: ☐ LEVEL ☐ UNLEVEL ☐ CONCRETE ☐ ROCK ☐ GRASS ☐ DIRT OTHER:	
SITE SIZE: ☐ TIGHT ☐ MODERATE ☐ SPACIOUS ☐ VERY LARGE	
TREES / SHADE: ☐ FULL SUN ☐ SOME SHADE ☐ A LOT OF SHADE	
FIRE RING / PIT: ☐ YES ☐ NO	FIRES ALLOWED: ☐ YES ☐ NO
PICNIC TABLE: ☐ YES ☐ NO	NICE VIEW: ☐ YES ☐ NO
CLOSE TO AMENITIES: ☐ YES ☐ NO	
NOISE:	
WILDLIFE:	
OTHER:	

DRAWING OF SITE OR FAVORITE PHOTO:

RV CAMPGROUND LOGBOOK

MANAGEMENT / BOOKING / CANCELLATION NOTES:

MANEUVERING / PARKING: ☐ TIGHT ROADS / TURNS   ☐ LOW-HANGING TREES   ☐ BAD ROAD CONDITIONS

OTHER PARKING NOTES:

SITE-SPECIFIC NOTES:	SITE NUMBER STAYED IN:

SITE HOOK UPS: ☐ FHU   ☐ W/E ONLY   ☐ 50 AMP   ☐ 30 AMP   ☐ DRY CAMPING

RV PAD: ☐ LEVEL ☐ UNLEVEL   ☐ CONCRETE   ☐ ROCK   ☐ GRASS   ☐ DIRT   OTHER:

SITE SIZE: ☐ TIGHT   ☐ MODERATE   ☐ SPACIOUS   ☐ VERY LARGE

TREES / SHADE: ☐ FULL SUN   ☐ SOME SHADE   ☐ A LOT OF SHADE

FIRE RING / PIT: ☐ YES ☐ NO	FIRES ALLOWED: ☐ YES ☐ NO
PICNIC TABLE: ☐ YES ☐ NO	NICE VIEW: ☐ YES ☐ NO

CLOSE TO AMENITIES: ☐ YES   ☐ NO

NOISE:

WILDLIFE:

OTHER:

DRAWING OF SITE OR FAVORITE PHOTO:

RV CAMPGROUND LOGBOOK

LOCAL AREA NOTES				

WEATHER DURING STAY: ☐ VERY COLD ☐ COLD ☐ MODERATE ☐ WARM ☐ HOT

OTHER WEATHER NOTES:

NEARBY SIGHTSEEING:

NEARBY RESTAURANTS:

NEARBY GROCERY STORE: ☐ 0-5 MIN. ☐ 5-10 MIN ☐ 10-20 MIN. ☐ 20-30 MIN. ☐ 30+ MIN.

OTHER GROCERY NOTES:

NEARBY PLACES VISITED:

VISIT / DO NEXT TIME:

DESTINATION: DATES:

TRAVELLED FROM: TO

VIA   MILEAGE

PREFERRED ROUTES / ROUTES TO AVOID:

SITES ALONG THE WAY:

WEATHER:

CAMPGROUND (NAME, LOCATION, CONTACT, FEES, RESERVATION)

CAMPGROUND PROS AND CONS:

CAMPSITE NUMBER AND DESCRIPTION:

THINGS TO AVOID NEXT TIME:

TRAVELLING COMPANIONS:

THINGS TO REMEMBER FOR NEXT TIME:

RV CAMPGROUND LOGBOOK

LOCAL AREA NOTES				
WEATHER DURING STAY: ☐ VERY COLD	☐ COLD	☐ MODERATE	☐ WARM	☐ HOT
OTHER WEATHER NOTES:				
NEARBY SIGHTSEEING:				
NEARBY RESTAURANTS:				
NEARBY GROCERY STORE: ☐ 0-5 MIN.	☐ 5-10 MIN	☐ 10-20 MIN.	☐ 20-30 MIN.	☐ 30+ MIN.
OTHER GROCERY NOTES:				
NEARBY PLACES VISITED:				
VISIT / DO NEXT TIME:				

DESTINATION:	DATES:
TRAVELLED FROM:	TO
VIA	MILEAGE
PREFERRED ROUTES / ROUTES TO AVOID:	
SITES ALONG THE WAY:	
WEATHER:	
CAMPGROUND (NAME, LOCATION, CONTACT, FEES, RESERVATION)	
CAMPGROUND PROS AND CONS:	
CAMPSITE NUMBER AND DESCRIPTION:	
THINGS TO AVOID NEXT TIME:	
TRAVELLING COMPANIONS:	
THINGS TO REMEMBER FOR NEXT TIME:	

RV PHOTO GALLERY

LOCATION		LOCATION	
	PHOTO		PHOTO
DATE:		DATE:	

LOCATION		LOCATION	
	PHOTO		PHOTO
DATE:		DATE:	

LOCATION		LOCATION	
	PHOTO		PHOTO
DATE:		DATE:	

NOTES	

RV PHOTO GALLERY

LOCATION		LOCATION	
PHOTO		PHOTO	
DATE:		DATE:	

LOCATION		LOCATION	
PHOTO		PHOTO	
DATE:		DATE:	

LOCATION		LOCATION	
PHOTO		PHOTO	
DATE:		DATE:	

NOTES	

DAILY RV PLANNER

	DESTINATION	ACTIVITIES
DAY 1		
DAY 2		
DAY 3		
DAY 4		
DAY 5		
DAY 6		
DAY 7		

DAILY RV PLANNER

	DESTINATION	ACTIVITIES
DAY 1		
DAY 2		
DAY 3		
DAY 4		
DAY 5		
DAY 6		
DAY 7		

WEEKLY RV SCHEDULE

LOCATION	SUN	MON	TUE	WED	THU	FRI	SAT

REMINDERS	LIST
○	○
○	○
○	○
○	○
○	○
○	○
○	○
○	○
○	○
○	○
○	○
○	

WEEKLY RV SCHEDULE

LOCATION	SUN	MON	TUE	WED	THU	FRI	SAT

REMINDERS	LIST
○	○
○	○
○	○
○	○
○	○
○	○
○	○
○	○
○	○
○	○
○	○
○	○

INDEX

RV LOGBOOK

CAMPGROUND:		DATE:
LOCATION:		
TRAVEL TO CAMPGROUND: MILES:	TIME:	COAST:
WEATHER:	TEMPERATURE:	

CAMPGROUND INFORMATION

NAME:	AMENITIES		
ADDRESS:	☐ SEWER	☐ PULL THROUGH	☐ BACK-IN
PHONE:	☐ PAVED	☐ PET FRIENDLY	☐ LAUNDRY
SITE:	☐ WATER	☐ EASY ACCESS	☐ ELECTRICITY
COAST:	☐ 15 AMP	☐ 30 AMP	☐ 50 AMP
	☐ SHADE	☐ POOL	☐ RESTROOMS
GPS:	☐ STORE	☐ PICNIC TABLE	☐ FIRE RING
RATING: ☆ ☆ ☆ ☆ ☆ ☆ ☆ ☆ ☆	☐ FIREWOOD	☐ TV	☐ WIFI

WATER PRESSURE	☆ ☆ ☆ ☆ ☆	☐ SECURITY	☐ ICE	☐ CAFE
CLEANLINESS	☆ ☆ ☆ ☆ ☆	ACTIVITIES		
LOCATION	☆ ☆ ☆ ☆ ☆	☐ FISHING	☐ SHUFFLEBOARD	☐ BOAT
SITE SIZE	☆ ☆ ☆ ☆ ☆	☐ LAKE	☐ PICKLEBALL	☐ GOLF
NOISE	☆ ☆ ☆ ☆ ☆	☐ BIKE	☐ CANOEING	☐ FITNESS
RESTROOMS	☆ ☆ ☆ ☆ ☆	☐ HIKING	☐ HOT TUB	☐ RIVER

CAMPED WITH		TO DO LIST	
		☐	
		☐	
		☐	
PEOPLE MET		☐	
		☐	
		☐	
		☐	
		☐	
PLACES VISITED		☐	
		☐	
		☐	

DATE LOG BOOK STARTED:	DATE LOG BOOK COMPLETED:

RV CAMPGROUND LOG

CAMPGROUND:			DATE:	
LOCATION:			RESERVATION NO.:	
CONTACT:			SITE NO.:	
WEBSITE:		NEARBY TOWN/CITY:		
DAILY RATE:	TOTAL:	ELECTRIC: ☐ 30 AMP ☐ 50 AMP	METER READING:	
DISCOUNT USED:	PET FRIENDLY: ☐ YES ☐ NO	DUMP STATION: ☐ SITE ☐ COMMUNITY ☐ HONEY DIPPER		

WIFI:
☐ EXCELLENT   ☐ GOOD   ☐ BAD   ☐ VERY BAD

WATER:
☐ EXCELLENT   ☐ GOOD   ☐ BAD   ☐ VERY BAD

NOTES:

NOTES:

FAVORITE SITES FOR NEXT VISIT:

POOL	SHOWERS	BIKE RENTALS	FISHING
HOT TUB	GROCERIES	BOAT RENTALS	RESTROOMS
CAMP STORE	LAUNDRY	NATURE TRAILS	HIKING
FITNESS ROOM	FIREWOOD	LAKE	ENTERTAINMENT

OTHER AMENITIES:

OTHER ACTIVITIES:

MOST MEMORABLE EVENT:

MOST FUN THINGS:

CAMPGROUND SCENERY:

WILDLIFE:

NOTES:

RV CAMPGROUND LOG

CAMPGROUND:		DATE:
LOCATION:		RESERVATION NO.:
CONTACT:		SITE NO.:

WEBSITE:	NEARBY TOWN/CITY:	

DAILY RATE:	TOTAL:	ELECTRIC: ☐ 30 AMP ☐ 50 AMP	METER READING:
DISCOUNT USED:	PET FRIENDLY: ☐ YES ☐ NO	DUMP STATION: ☐ SITE ☐ COMMUNITY ☐ HONEY DIPPER	

WIFI: ☐ EXCELLENT ☐ GOOD ☐ BAD ☐ VERY BAD	WATER: ☐ EXCELLENT ☐ GOOD ☐ BAD ☐ VERY BAD
NOTES:	NOTES:

FAVORITE SITES FOR NEXT VISIT:

POOL	SHOWERS	BIKE RENTALS	FISHING
HOT TUB	GROCERIES	BOAT RENTALS	RESTROOMS
CAMP STORE	LAUNDRY	NATURE TRAILS	HIKING
FITNESS ROOM	FIREWOOD	LAKE	ENTERTAINMENT

OTHER AMENITIES:

OTHER ACTIVITIES:

MOST MEMORABLE EVENT:

MOST FUN THINGS:

CAMPGROUND SCENERY:

WILDLIFE:

NOTES:

RV CAMPGROUND LOGBOOK

MANAGEMENT / BOOKING / CANCELLATION NOTES:

MANEUVERING / PARKING: ☐ TIGHT ROADS / TURNS   ☐ LOW-HANGING TREES   ☐ BAD ROAD CONDITIONS

OTHER PARKING NOTES:

SITE-SPECIFIC NOTES:	SITE NUMBER STAYED IN:

SITE HOOK UPS: ☐ FHU   ☐ W/E ONLY   ☐ 50 AMP   ☐ 30 AMP   ☐ DRY CAMPING

RV PAD: ☐ LEVEL ☐ UNLEVEL   ☐ CONCRETE   ☐ ROCK   ☐ GRASS   ☐ DIRT   OTHER:

SITE SIZE: ☐ TIGHT   ☐ MODERATE   ☐ SPACIOUS   ☐ VERY LARGE

TREES / SHADE: ☐ FULL SUN   ☐ SOME SHADE   ☐ A LOT OF SHADE

FIRE RING / PIT: ☐ YES ☐ NO	FIRES ALLOWED: ☐ YES ☐ NO
PICNIC TABLE: ☐ YES ☐ NO	NICE VIEW: ☐ YES ☐ NO

CLOSE TO AMENITIES: ☐ YES   ☐ NO

NOISE:

WILDLIFE:

OTHER:

DRAWING OF SITE OR FAVORITE PHOTO:

RV CAMPGROUND LOGBOOK

MANAGEMENT / BOOKING / CANCELLATION NOTES:

MANEUVERING / PARKING: ☐ TIGHT ROADS / TURNS   ☐ LOW-HANGING TREES   ☐ BAD ROAD CONDITIONS

OTHER PARKING NOTES:

SITE-SPECIFIC NOTES: SITE NUMBER STAYED IN:

SITE HOOK UPS: ☐ FHU   ☐ W/E ONLY   ☐ 50 AMP   ☐ 30 AMP   ☐ DRY CAMPING

RV PAD: ☐ LEVEL ☐ UNLEVEL   ☐ CONCRETE   ☐ ROCK   ☐ GRASS   ☐ DIRT   OTHER:

SITE SIZE: ☐ TIGHT   ☐ MODERATE   ☐ SPACIOUS   ☐ VERY LARGE

TREES / SHADE: ☐ FULL SUN   ☐ SOME SHADE   ☐ A LOT OF SHADE

FIRE RING / PIT: ☐ YES   ☐ NO   FIRES ALLOWED: ☐ YES   ☐ NO

PICNIC TABLE: ☐ YES   ☐ NO   NICE VIEW: ☐ YES   ☐ NO

CLOSE TO AMENITIES: ☐ YES   ☐ NO

NOISE:

WILDLIFE:

OTHER:

DRAWING OF SITE OR FAVORITE PHOTO:

RV CAMPGROUND LOGBOOK

LOCAL AREA NOTES				
WEATHER DURING STAY: ☐ VERY COLD	☐ COLD	☐ MODERATE	☐ WARM	☐ HOT
OTHER WEATHER NOTES:				
NEARBY SIGHTSEEING:				
NEARBY RESTAURANTS:				
NEARBY GROCERY STORE: ☐ 0-5 MIN.	☐ 5-10 MIN	☐ 10-20 MIN.	☐ 20-30 MIN.	☐ 30+ MIN.
OTHER GROCERY NOTES:				
NEARBY PLACES VISITED:				
VISIT / DO NEXT TIME:				

DESTINATION:	DATES:
TRAVELLED FROM:	TO
VIA	MILEAGE

PREFERRED ROUTES / ROUTES TO AVOID:

SITES ALONG THE WAY:

WEATHER:

CAMPGROUND (NAME, LOCATION, CONTACT, FEES, RESERVATION)

CAMPGROUND PROS AND CONS:

CAMPSITE NUMBER AND DESCRIPTION:

THINGS TO AVOID NEXT TIME:

TRAVELLING COMPANIONS:

THINGS TO REMEMBER FOR NEXT TIME:

RV CAMPGROUND LOGBOOK

LOCAL AREA NOTES					
WEATHER DURING STAY:	☐ VERY COLD	☐ COLD	☐ MODERATE	☐ WARM	☐ HOT
OTHER WEATHER NOTES:					
NEARBY SIGHTSEEING:					
NEARBY RESTAURANTS:					
NEARBY GROCERY STORE:	☐ 0-5 MIN.	☐ 5-10 MIN	☐ 10-20 MIN.	☐ 20-30 MIN.	☐ 30+ MIN.
OTHER GROCERY NOTES:					
NEARBY PLACES VISITED:					
VISIT / DO NEXT TIME:					

DESTINATION:	DATES:
TRAVELLED FROM:	TO
VIA	MILEAGE
PREFERRED ROUTES / ROUTES TO AVOID:	
SITES ALONG THE WAY:	
WEATHER:	
CAMPGROUND (NAME, LOCATION, CONTACT, FEES, RESERVATION)	
CAMPGROUND PROS AND CONS:	
CAMPSITE NUMBER AND DESCRIPTION:	
THINGS TO AVOID NEXT TIME:	
TRAVELLING COMPANIONS:	
THINGS TO REMEMBER FOR NEXT TIME:	

RV PHOTO GALLERY

LOCATION	LOCATION
PHOTO	PHOTO
DATE:	DATE:

LOCATION	LOCATION
PHOTO	PHOTO
DATE:	DATE:

LOCATION	LOCATION
PHOTO	PHOTO
DATE:	DATE:

NOTES

RV PHOTO GALLERY

LOCATION		LOCATION	
	PHOTO		PHOTO
DATE:		DATE:	

LOCATION		LOCATION	
	PHOTO		PHOTO
DATE:		DATE:	

LOCATION		LOCATION	
	PHOTO		PHOTO
DATE:		DATE:	

NOTES

DAILY RV PLANNER

	DESTINATION	ACTIVITIES
DAY 1		
DAY 2		
DAY 3		
DAY 4		
DAY 5		
DAY 6		
DAY 7		

DAILY RV PLANNER

	DESTINATION	ACTIVITIES
DAY 1		
DAY 2		
DAY 3		
DAY 4		
DAY 5		
DAY 6		
DAY 7		

WEEKLY RV SCHEDULE

LOCATION	SUN	MON	TUE	WED	THU	FRI	SAT

REMINDERS	LIST
○	○
○	○
○	○
○	○
○	○
○	○
○	○
○	○
○	○
○	○
○	○
○	○

WEEKLY RV SCHEDULE

LOCATION	SUN	MON	TUE	WED	THU	FRI	SAT

REMINDERS	LIST
○	○
○	○
○	○
○	○
○	○
○	○
○	○
○	○
○	○
○	○
○	○
○	○

INDEX

RV LOGBOOK

CAMPGROUND:	DATE:
LOCATION:	

TRAVEL TO CAMPGROUND: MILES:	TIME:	COAST:

WEATHER:	TEMPERATURE:

CAMPGROUND INFORMATION

NAME:	AMENITIES		
ADDRESS:	☐ SEWER	☐ PULL THROUGH	☐ BACK-IN
PHONE:	☐ PAVED	☐ PET FRIENDLY	☐ LAUNDRY
SITE:	☐ WATER	☐ EASY ACCESS	☐ ELECTRICITY
COAST:	☐ 15 AMP	☐ 30 AMP	☐ 50 AMP
	☐ SHADE	☐ POOL	☐ RESTROOMS
GPS:	☐ STORE	☐ PICNIC TABLE	☐ FIRE RING
RATING:☆ ☆ ☆ ☆ ☆ ☆ ☆ ☆ ☆	☐ FIREWOOD	☐ TV	☐ WIFI

WATER PRESSURE	☆ ☆ ☆ ☆ ☆	☐ SECURITY	☐ ICE	☐ CAFE
CLEANLINESS	☆ ☆ ☆ ☆ ☆	ACTIVITIES		
LOCATION	☆ ☆ ☆ ☆ ☆	☐ FISHING	☐ SHUFFLEBOARD	☐ BOAT
SITE SIZE	☆ ☆ ☆ ☆ ☆	☐ LAKE	☐ PICKLEBALL	☐ GOLF
NOISE	☆ ☆ ☆ ☆ ☆	☐ BIKE	☐ CANOEING	☐ FITNESS
RESTROOMS	☆ ☆ ☆ ☆ ☆	☐ HIKING	☐ HOT TUB	☐ RIVER

CAMPED WITH		TO DO LIST
		☐
		☐
		☐
PEOPLE MET		☐
		☐
		☐
		☐
		☐
PLACES VISITED		☐
		☐
		☐

DATE LOG BOOK STARTED:	DATE LOG BOOK COMPLETED:

RV CAMPGROUND LOG

CAMPGROUND:			DATE:	
LOCATION:			RESERVATION NO.:	
CONTACT:			SITE NO.:	
WEBSITE:		NEARBY TOWN/CITY:		
DAILY RATE:	TOTAL:	ELECTRIC: ☐ 30 AMP ☐ 50 AMP		METER READING:
DISCOUNT USED:	PET FRIENDLY: ☐ YES ☐ NO	DUMP STATION: ☐ SITE ☐ COMMUNITY ☐ HONEY DIPPER		
WIFI: ☐ EXCELLENT ☐ GOOD ☐ BAD ☐ VERY BAD		WATER: ☐ EXCELLENT ☐ GOOD ☐ BAD ☐ VERY BAD		
NOTES:		NOTES:		

FAVORITE SITES FOR NEXT VISIT:

POOL	SHOWERS	BIKE RENTALS	FISHING
HOT TUB	GROCERIES	BOAT RENTALS	RESTROOMS
CAMP STORE	LAUNDRY	NATURE TRAILS	HIKING
FITNESS ROOM	FIREWOOD	LAKE	ENTERTAINMENT

OTHER AMENITIES:

OTHER ACTIVITIES:

MOST MEMORABLE EVENT:

MOST FUN THINGS:

CAMPGROUND SCENERY:

WILDLIFE:

NOTES:

RV CAMPGROUND LOG

CAMPGROUND:	DATE:
LOCATION:	RESERVATION NO.:
CONTACT:	SITE NO.:

WEBSITE:		NEARBY TOWN/CITY:	
DAILY RATE:	TOTAL:	ELECTRIC: ☐ 30 AMP ☐ 50 AMP	METER READING:
DISCOUNT USED:	PET FRIENDLY: ☐ YES ☐ NO	DUMP STATION: ☐ SITE ☐ COMMUNITY ☐ HONEY DIPPER	

WIFI: ☐ EXCELLENT ☐ GOOD ☐ BAD ☐ VERY BAD	WATER: ☐ EXCELLENT ☐ GOOD ☐ BAD ☐ VERY BAD
NOTES:	NOTES:

FAVORITE SITES FOR NEXT VISIT:

POOL	SHOWERS	BIKE RENTALS	FISHING
HOT TUB	GROCERIES	BOAT RENTALS	RESTROOMS
CAMP STORE	LAUNDRY	NATURE TRAILS	HIKING
FITNESS ROOM	FIREWOOD	LAKE	ENTERTAINMENT

OTHER AMENITIES:

OTHER ACTIVITIES:

MOST MEMORABLE EVENT:

MOST FUN THINGS:

CAMPGROUND SCENERY:

WILDLIFE:

NOTES:

RV CAMPGROUND LOGBOOK

MANAGEMENT / BOOKING / CANCELLATION NOTES:

MANEUVERING / PARKING: ☐ TIGHT ROADS / TURNS   ☐ LOW-HANGING TREES   ☐ BAD ROAD CONDITIONS

OTHER PARKING NOTES:

SITE-SPECIFIC NOTES: | SITE NUMBER STAYED IN:

SITE HOOK UPS: ☐ FHU   ☐ W/E ONLY   ☐ 50 AMP   ☐ 30 AMP   ☐ DRY CAMPING

RV PAD: ☐ LEVEL ☐ UNLEVEL   ☐ CONCRETE   ☐ ROCK   ☐ GRASS   ☐ DIRT   OTHER:

SITE SIZE: ☐ TIGHT   ☐ MODERATE   ☐ SPACIOUS   ☐ VERY LARGE

TREES / SHADE: ☐ FULL SUN   ☐ SOME SHADE   ☐ A LOT OF SHADE

FIRE RING / PIT: ☐ YES   ☐ NO   FIRES ALLOWED: ☐ YES   ☐ NO

PICNIC TABLE: ☐ YES   ☐ NO   NICE VIEW: ☐ YES   ☐ NO

CLOSE TO AMENITIES: ☐ YES   ☐ NO

NOISE:

WILDLIFE:

OTHER:

DRAWING OF SITE OR FAVORITE PHOTO:

RV CAMPGROUND LOGBOOK

MANAGEMENT / BOOKING / CANCELLATION NOTES:

MANEUVERING / PARKING: ☐ TIGHT ROADS / TURNS   ☐ LOW-HANGING TREES   ☐ BAD ROAD CONDITIONS

OTHER PARKING NOTES:

SITE-SPECIFIC NOTES:	SITE NUMBER STAYED IN:

SITE HOOK UPS: ☐ FHU   ☐ W/E ONLY   ☐ 50 AMP   ☐ 30 AMP   ☐ DRY CAMPING

RV PAD: ☐ LEVEL ☐ UNLEVEL   ☐ CONCRETE   ☐ ROCK   ☐ GRASS   ☐ DIRT   OTHER:

SITE SIZE: ☐ TIGHT   ☐ MODERATE   ☐ SPACIOUS   ☐ VERY LARGE

TREES / SHADE: ☐ FULL SUN   ☐ SOME SHADE   ☐ A LOT OF SHADE

FIRE RING / PIT: ☐ YES ☐ NO	FIRES ALLOWED: ☐ YES ☐ NO
PICNIC TABLE: ☐ YES ☐ NO	NICE VIEW: ☐ YES ☐ NO

CLOSE TO AMENITIES: ☐ YES   ☐ NO

NOISE:

WILDLIFE:

OTHER:

DRAWING OF SITE OR FAVORITE PHOTO:

RV CAMPGROUND LOGBOOK

LOCAL AREA NOTES				
WEATHER DURING STAY: ☐ VERY COLD	☐ COLD	☐ MODERATE	☐ WARM	☐ HOT
OTHER WEATHER NOTES:				
NEARBY SIGHTSEEING:				
NEARBY RESTAURANTS:				
NEARBY GROCERY STORE: ☐ 0-5 MIN.	☐ 5-10 MIN	☐ 10-20 MIN.	☐ 20-30 MIN.	☐ 30+ MIN.
OTHER GROCERY NOTES:				
NEARBY PLACES VISITED:				
VISIT / DO NEXT TIME:				

DESTINATION:	DATES:
TRAVELLED FROM:	TO
VIA	MILEAGE
PREFERRED ROUTES / ROUTES TO AVOID:	
SITES ALONG THE WAY:	
WEATHER:	
CAMPGROUND (NAME, LOCATION, CONTACT, FEES, RESERVATION)	
CAMPGROUND PROS AND CONS:	
CAMPSITE NUMBER AND DESCRIPTION:	
THINGS TO AVOID NEXT TIME:	
TRAVELLING COMPANIONS:	
THINGS TO REMEMBER FOR NEXT TIME:	

RV CAMPGROUND LOGBOOK

LOCAL AREA NOTES				
WEATHER DURING STAY:	☐ VERY COLD	☐ COLD	☐ MODERATE	☐ WARM ☐ HOT

OTHER WEATHER NOTES:

NEARBY SIGHTSEEING:

NEARBY RESTAURANTS:

NEARBY GROCERY STORE:	☐ 0-5 MIN.	☐ 5-10 MIN	☐ 10-20 MIN.	☐ 20-30 MIN.	☐ 30+ MIN.

OTHER GROCERY NOTES:

NEARBY PLACES VISITED:

VISIT / DO NEXT TIME:

DESTINATION:	DATES:
TRAVELLED FROM:	TO
VIA	MILEAGE

PREFERRED ROUTES / ROUTES TO AVOID:

SITES ALONG THE WAY:

WEATHER:

CAMPGROUND (NAME, LOCATION, CONTACT, FEES, RESERVATION)

CAMPGROUND PROS AND CONS:

CAMPSITE NUMBER AND DESCRIPTION:

THINGS TO AVOID NEXT TIME:

TRAVELLING COMPANIONS:

THINGS TO REMEMBER FOR NEXT TIME:

RV PHOTO GALLERY

LOCATION		LOCATION	
	PHOTO		PHOTO
DATE:		DATE:	

LOCATION		LOCATION	
	PHOTO		PHOTO
DATE:		DATE:	

LOCATION		LOCATION	
	PHOTO		PHOTO
DATE:		DATE:	

NOTES	

RV PHOTO GALLERY

LOCATION		LOCATION	
PHOTO		PHOTO	
DATE:		DATE:	

LOCATION		LOCATION	
PHOTO		PHOTO	
DATE:		DATE:	

LOCATION		LOCATION	
PHOTO		PHOTO	
DATE:		DATE:	

NOTES

DAILY RV PLANNER

	DESTINATION	ACTIVITIES
DAY 1		
DAY 2		
DAY 3		
DAY 4		
DAY 5		
DAY 6		
DAY 7		

DAILY RV PLANNER

	DESTINATION	ACTIVITIES
DAY 1		
DAY 2		
DAY 3		
DAY 4		
DAY 5		
DAY 6		
DAY 7		

WEEKLY RV SCHEDULE

LOCATION	SUN	MON	TUE	WED	THU	FRI	SAT

REMINDERS	LIST
○	○
○	○
○	○
○	○
○	○
○	○
○	○
○	○
○	○
○	○
○	○
○	○

WEEKLY RV SCHEDULE

LOCATION	SUN	MON	TUE	WED	THU	FRI	SAT

REMINDERS	LIST
○	○
○	○
○	○
○	○
○	○
○	○
○	○
○	○
○	○
○	○
○	○
○	○

INDEX

RV LOGBOOK

CAMPGROUND:		DATE:
LOCATION:		
TRAVEL TO CAMPGROUND: MILES:	TIME:	COAST:
WEATHER:	TEMPERATURE:	

CAMPGROUND INFORMATION

NAME:	AMENITIES		
ADDRESS:	☐ SEWER	☐ PULL THROUGH	☐ BACK-IN
PHONE:	☐ PAVED	☐ PET FRIENDLY	☐ LAUNDRY
SITE:	☐ WATER	☐ EASY ACCESS	☐ ELECTRICITY
COAST:	☐ 15 AMP	☐ 30 AMP	☐ 50 AMP
	☐ SHADE	☐ POOL	☐ RESTROOMS
GPS:	☐ STORE	☐ PICNIC TABLE	☐ FIRE RING
RATING: ☆ ☆ ☆ ☆ ☆ ☆ ☆ ☆ ☆ ☆	☐ FIREWOOD	☐ TV	☐ WIFI
	☐ SECURITY	☐ ICE	☐ CAFE

WATER PRESSURE	☆ ☆ ☆ ☆ ☆
CLEANLINESS	☆ ☆ ☆ ☆ ☆
LOCATION	☆ ☆ ☆ ☆ ☆
SITE SIZE	☆ ☆ ☆ ☆ ☆
NOISE	☆ ☆ ☆ ☆ ☆
RESTROOMS	☆ ☆ ☆ ☆ ☆

ACTIVITIES		
☐ FISHING	☐ SHUFFLEBOARD	☐ BOAT
☐ LAKE	☐ PICKLEBALL	☐ GOLF
☐ BIKE	☐ CANOEING	☐ FITNESS
☐ HIKING	☐ HOT TUB	☐ RIVER

CAMPED WITH		TO DO LIST
		☐
		☐
		☐
PEOPLE MET		☐
		☐
		☐
		☐
		☐
PLACES VISITED		☐
		☐
		☐

DATE LOG BOOK STARTED:	DATE LOG BOOK COMPLETED:

RV CAMPGROUND LOG

CAMPGROUND:			DATE:
LOCATION:			RESERVATION NO.:
CONTACT:			SITE NO.:

| WEBSITE: | | NEARBY TOWN/CITY: | |

| DAILY RATE: | TOTAL: | ELECTRIC:
☐ 30 AMP ☐ 50 AMP | METER READING: |
| DISCOUNT USED: | PET FRIENDLY:
☐ YES   ☐ NO | DUMP STATION:
☐ SITE   ☐ COMMUNITY   ☐ HONEY DIPPER | |

| WIFI:
☐ EXCELLENT   ☐ GOOD   ☐ BAD   ☐ VERY BAD | WATER:
☐ EXCELLENT   ☐ GOOD   ☐ BAD   ☐ VERY BAD |
| NOTES: | NOTES: |

FAVORITE SITES FOR NEXT VISIT:

POOL	SHOWERS	BIKE RENTALS	FISHING
HOT TUB	GROCERIES	BOAT RENTALS	RESTROOMS
CAMP STORE	LAUNDRY	NATURE TRAILS	HIKING
FITNESS ROOM	FIREWOOD	LAKE	ENTERTAINMENT

OTHER AMENITIES:

OTHER ACTIVITIES:

MOST MEMORABLE EVENT:

MOST FUN THINGS:

CAMPGROUND SCENERY:

WILDLIFE:

NOTES:

RV CAMPGROUND LOG

CAMPGROUND:		DATE:

LOCATION:		RESERVATION NO.:

CONTACT:		SITE NO.:

WEBSITE:	NEARBY TOWN/CITY:

DAILY RATE:	TOTAL:	ELECTRIC: ☐ 30 AMP ☐ 50 AMP	METER READING:

DISCOUNT USED:	PET FRIENDLY: ☐ YES ☐ NO	DUMP STATION: ☐ SITE ☐ COMMUNITY ☐ HONEY DIPPER

WIFI: ☐ EXCELLENT ☐ GOOD ☐ BAD ☐ VERY BAD	WATER: ☐ EXCELLENT ☐ GOOD ☐ BAD ☐ VERY BAD

NOTES:	NOTES:

FAVORITE SITES FOR NEXT VISIT:

POOL	SHOWERS	BIKE RENTALS	FISHING
HOT TUB	GROCERIES	BOAT RENTALS	RESTROOMS
CAMP STORE	LAUNDRY	NATURE TRAILS	HIKING
FITNESS ROOM	FIREWOOD	LAKE	ENTERTAINMENT

OTHER AMENITIES:

OTHER ACTIVITIES:

MOST MEMORABLE EVENT:

MOST FUN THINGS:

CAMPGROUND SCENERY:

WILDLIFE:

NOTES:

RV CAMPGROUND LOGBOOK

MANAGEMENT / BOOKING / CANCELLATION NOTES:

MANEUVERING / PARKING: ☐ TIGHT ROADS / TURNS   ☐ LOW-HANGING TREES   ☐ BAD ROAD CONDITIONS

OTHER PARKING NOTES:

SITE-SPECIFIC NOTES:

SITE NUMBER STAYED IN:

SITE HOOK UPS: ☐ FHU   ☐ W/E ONLY   ☐ 50 AMP   ☐ 30 AMP   ☐ DRY CAMPING

RV PAD: ☐ LEVEL ☐ UNLEVEL   ☐ CONCRETE   ☐ ROCK   ☐ GRASS   ☐ DIRT   OTHER:

SITE SIZE: ☐ TIGHT   ☐ MODERATE   ☐ SPACIOUS   ☐ VERY LARGE

TREES / SHADE: ☐ FULL SUN   ☐ SOME SHADE   ☐ A LOT OF SHADE

FIRE RING / PIT: ☐ YES   ☐ NO   FIRES ALLOWED: ☐ YES   ☐ NO

PICNIC TABLE: ☐ YES   ☐ NO   NICE VIEW: ☐ YES   ☐ NO

CLOSE TO AMENITIES: ☐ YES   ☐ NO

NOISE:

WILDLIFE:

OTHER:

DRAWING OF SITE OR FAVORITE PHOTO:

RV CAMPGROUND LOGBOOK

MANAGEMENT / BOOKING / CANCELLATION NOTES:

MANEUVERING / PARKING: ☐ TIGHT ROADS / TURNS   ☐ LOW-HANGING TREES   ☐ BAD ROAD CONDITIONS

OTHER PARKING NOTES:

SITE-SPECIFIC NOTES:	SITE NUMBER STAYED IN:

SITE HOOK UPS: ☐ FHU   ☐ W/E ONLY   ☐ 50 AMP   ☐ 30 AMP   ☐ DRY CAMPING

RV PAD: ☐ LEVEL ☐ UNLEVEL   ☐ CONCRETE   ☐ ROCK   ☐ GRASS   ☐ DIRT   OTHER:

SITE SIZE: ☐ TIGHT   ☐ MODERATE   ☐ SPACIOUS   ☐ VERY LARGE

TREES / SHADE: ☐ FULL SUN   ☐ SOME SHADE   ☐ A LOT OF SHADE

FIRE RING / PIT: ☐ YES ☐ NO	FIRES ALLOWED: ☐ YES ☐ NO
PICNIC TABLE: ☐ YES ☐ NO	NICE VIEW: ☐ YES ☐ NO

CLOSE TO AMENITIES: ☐ YES   ☐ NO

NOISE:

WILDLIFE:

OTHER:

DRAWING OF SITE OR FAVORITE PHOTO:

RV CAMPGROUND LOGBOOK

LOCAL AREA NOTES				
WEATHER DURING STAY:	☐ VERY COLD	☐ COLD	☐ MODERATE	☐ WARM ☐ HOT

OTHER WEATHER NOTES:

NEARBY SIGHTSEEING:

NEARBY RESTAURANTS:

NEARBY GROCERY STORE:	☐ 0-5 MIN.	☐ 5-10 MIN	☐ 10-20 MIN.	☐ 20-30 MIN.	☐ 30+ MIN.

OTHER GROCERY NOTES:

NEARBY PLACES VISITED:

VISIT / DO NEXT TIME:

DESTINATION: | DATES:

TRAVELLED FROM: | TO

VIA | MILEAGE

PREFERRED ROUTES / ROUTES TO AVOID:

SITES ALONG THE WAY:

WEATHER:

CAMPGROUND (NAME, LOCATION, CONTACT, FEES, RESERVATION)

CAMPGROUND PROS AND CONS:

CAMPSITE NUMBER AND DESCRIPTION:

THINGS TO AVOID NEXT TIME:

TRAVELLING COMPANIONS:

THINGS TO REMEMBER FOR NEXT TIME:

RV CAMPGROUND LOGBOOK

LOCAL AREA NOTES				
WEATHER DURING STAY: ☐ VERY COLD	☐ COLD	☐ MODERATE	☐ WARM	☐ HOT
OTHER WEATHER NOTES:				
NEARBY SIGHTSEEING:				
NEARBY RESTAURANTS:				
NEARBY GROCERY STORE: ☐ 0-5 MIN.	☐ 5-10 MIN	☐ 10-20 MIN.	☐ 20-30 MIN.	☐ 30+ MIN.
OTHER GROCERY NOTES:				
NEARBY PLACES VISITED:				
VISIT / DO NEXT TIME:				

DESTINATION:	DATES:
TRAVELLED FROM:	TO
VIA	MILEAGE
PREFERRED ROUTES / ROUTES TO AVOID:	
SITES ALONG THE WAY:	
WEATHER:	
CAMPGROUND (NAME, LOCATION, CONTACT, FEES, RESERVATION)	
CAMPGROUND PROS AND CONS:	
CAMPSITE NUMBER AND DESCRIPTION:	
THINGS TO AVOID NEXT TIME:	
TRAVELLING COMPANIONS:	
THINGS TO REMEMBER FOR NEXT TIME:	

RV PHOTO GALLERY

LOCATION		LOCATION	
	PHOTO		PHOTO
DATE:		DATE:	

LOCATION		LOCATION	
	PHOTO		PHOTO
DATE:		DATE:	

LOCATION		LOCATION	
	PHOTO		PHOTO
DATE:		DATE:	

NOTES	

RV PHOTO GALLERY

LOCATION		LOCATION	
	PHOTO		PHOTO
DATE:		DATE:	

LOCATION		LOCATION	
	PHOTO		PHOTO
DATE:		DATE:	

LOCATION		LOCATION	
	PHOTO		PHOTO
DATE:		DATE:	

NOTES	

DAILY RV PLANNER

	DESTINATION	ACTIVITIES
DAY 1		
DAY 2		
DAY 3		
DAY 4		
DAY 5		
DAY 6		
DAY 7		

DAILY RV PLANNER

	DESTINATION	ACTIVITIES
DAY 1		
DAY 2		
DAY 3		
DAY 4		
DAY 5		
DAY 6		
DAY 7		

WEEKLY RV SCHEDULE

LOCATION	SUN	MON	TUE	WED	THU	FRI	SAT

REMINDERS	LIST
○	○
○	○
○	○
○	○
○	○
○	○
○	○
○	○
○	○
○	○
○	○

WEEKLY RV SCHEDULE

LOCATION	SUN	MON	TUE	WED	THU	FRI	SAT

REMINDERS	LIST
○	○
○	○
○	○
○	○
○	○
○	○
○	○
○	○
○	○
○	○
○	○
○	○

INDEX

RV LOGBOOK

CAMPGROUND:		DATE:
LOCATION:		
TRAVEL TO CAMPGROUND: MILES:	TIME:	COAST:
WEATHER:	TEMPERATURE:	

CAMPGROUND INFORMATION

NAME:			
ADDRESS:		AMENITIES	
	□ SEWER	□ PULL THROUGH	□ BACK-IN
PHONE:	□ PAVED	□ PET FRIENDLY	□ LAUNDRY
SITE:	□ WATER	□ EASY ACCESS	□ ELECTRICITY
COAST:	□ 15 AMP	□ 30 AMP	□ 50 AMP
	□ SHADE	□ POOL	□ RESTROOMS
GPS:	□ STORE	□ PICNIC TABLE	□ FIRE RING
RATING: ☆ ☆ ☆ ☆ ☆ ☆ ☆ ☆ ☆ ☆	□ FIREWOOD	□ TV	□ WIFI

WATER PRESSURE	☆ ☆ ☆ ☆ ☆
CLEANLINESS	☆ ☆ ☆ ☆ ☆
LOCATION	☆ ☆ ☆ ☆ ☆
SITE SIZE	☆ ☆ ☆ ☆ ☆
NOISE	☆ ☆ ☆ ☆ ☆
RESTROOMS	☆ ☆ ☆ ☆ ☆

□ SECURITY	□ ICE	□ CAFE

ACTIVITIES		
□ FISHING	□ SHUFFLEBOARD	□ BOAT
□ LAKE	□ PICKLEBALL	□ GOLF
□ BIKE	□ CANOEING	□ FITNESS
□ HIKING	□ HOT TUB	□ RIVER

CAMPED WITH		TO DO LIST
		□
		□
		□
PEOPLE MET		□
		□
		□
		□
		□
PLACES VISITED		□
		□
		□

DATE LOG BOOK STARTED:	DATE LOG BOOK COMPLETED:

RV CAMPGROUND LOG

CAMPGROUND:			DATE:	
LOCATION:			RESERVATION NO.:	
CONTACT:			SITE NO.:	
WEBSITE:		NEARBY TOWN/CITY:		
DAILY RATE:	TOTAL:	ELECTRIC: ☐ 30 AMP ☐ 50 AMP		METER READING:
DISCOUNT USED:	PET FRIENDLY: ☐ YES ☐ NO	DUMP STATION: ☐ SITE ☐ COMMUNITY ☐ HONEY DIPPER		

WIFI:
☐ EXCELLENT   ☐ GOOD   ☐ BAD   ☐ VERY BAD

WATER:
☐ EXCELLENT   ☐ GOOD   ☐ BAD   ☐ VERY BAD

NOTES:

NOTES:

FAVORITE SITES FOR NEXT VISIT:

POOL	SHOWERS	BIKE RENTALS	FISHING
HOT TUB	GROCERIES	BOAT RENTALS	RESTROOMS
CAMP STORE	LAUNDRY	NATURE TRAILS	HIKING
FITNESS ROOM	FIREWOOD	LAKE	ENTERTAINMENT

OTHER AMENITIES:

OTHER ACTIVITIES:

MOST MEMORABLE EVENT:

MOST FUN THINGS:

CAMPGROUND SCENERY:

WILDLIFE:

NOTES:

RV CAMPGROUND LOG

CAMPGROUND:		DATE:
LOCATION:		RESERVATION NO.:
CONTACT:		SITE NO.:

WEBSITE:		NEARBY TOWN/CITY:	

DAILY RATE:	TOTAL:	ELECTRIC: ☐ 30 AMP ☐ 50 AMP	METER READING:
DISCOUNT USED:	PET FRIENDLY: ☐ YES ☐ NO	DUMP STATION: ☐ SITE ☐ COMMUNITY ☐ HONEY DIPPER	

WIFI: ☐ EXCELLENT ☐ GOOD ☐ BAD ☐ VERY BAD	WATER: ☐ EXCELLENT ☐ GOOD ☐ BAD ☐ VERY BAD
NOTES:	NOTES:

FAVORITE SITES FOR NEXT VISIT:

POOL	SHOWERS	BIKE RENTALS	FISHING
HOT TUB	GROCERIES	BOAT RENTALS	RESTROOMS
CAMP STORE	LAUNDRY	NATURE TRAILS	HIKING
FITNESS ROOM	FIREWOOD	LAKE	ENTERTAINMENT

OTHER AMENITIES:

OTHER ACTIVITIES:

MOST MEMORABLE EVENT:

MOST FUN THINGS:

CAMPGROUND SCENERY:

WILDLIFE:

NOTES:

RV CAMPGROUND LOGBOOK

MANAGEMENT / BOOKING / CANCELLATION NOTES:

MANEUVERING / PARKING: ☐ TIGHT ROADS / TURNS   ☐ LOW-HANGING TREES   ☐ BAD ROAD CONDITIONS

OTHER PARKING NOTES:

SITE-SPECIFIC NOTES:	SITE NUMBER STAYED IN:

SITE HOOK UPS: ☐ FHU   ☐ W/E ONLY   ☐ 50 AMP   ☐ 30 AMP   ☐ DRY CAMPING

RV PAD: ☐ LEVEL ☐ UNLEVEL   ☐ CONCRETE   ☐ ROCK   ☐ GRASS   ☐ DIRT   OTHER:

SITE SIZE: ☐ TIGHT   ☐ MODERATE   ☐ SPACIOUS   ☐ VERY LARGE

TREES / SHADE: ☐ FULL SUN   ☐ SOME SHADE   ☐ A LOT OF SHADE

FIRE RING / PIT: ☐ YES   ☐ NO   FIRES ALLOWED: ☐ YES   ☐ NO

PICNIC TABLE: ☐ YES   ☐ NO   NICE VIEW: ☐ YES   ☐ NO

CLOSE TO AMENITIES: ☐ YES   ☐ NO

NOISE:

WILDLIFE:

OTHER:

DRAWING OF SITE OR FAVORITE PHOTO:

RV CAMPGROUND LOGBOOK

MANAGEMENT / BOOKING / CANCELLATION NOTES:

MANEUVERING / PARKING: ☐ TIGHT ROADS / TURNS   ☐ LOW-HANGING TREES   ☐ BAD ROAD CONDITIONS

OTHER PARKING NOTES:

SITE-SPECIFIC NOTES: | SITE NUMBER STAYED IN:

SITE HOOK UPS: ☐ FHU   ☐ W/E ONLY   ☐ 50 AMP   ☐ 30 AMP   ☐ DRY CAMPING

RV PAD: ☐ LEVEL ☐ UNLEVEL   ☐ CONCRETE   ☐ ROCK   ☐ GRASS   ☐ DIRT   OTHER:

SITE SIZE: ☐ TIGHT   ☐ MODERATE   ☐ SPACIOUS   ☐ VERY LARGE

TREES / SHADE: ☐ FULL SUN   ☐ SOME SHADE   ☐ A LOT OF SHADE

FIRE RING / PIT: ☐ YES   ☐ NO   FIRES ALLOWED: ☐ YES   ☐ NO

PICNIC TABLE: ☐ YES   ☐ NO   NICE VIEW: ☐ YES   ☐ NO

CLOSE TO AMENITIES: ☐ YES   ☐ NO

NOISE:

WILDLIFE:

OTHER:

DRAWING OF SITE OR FAVORITE PHOTO:

RV CAMPGROUND LOGBOOK

LOCAL AREA NOTES				
WEATHER DURING STAY: ☐ VERY COLD	☐ COLD	☐ MODERATE	☐ WARM	☐ HOT

OTHER WEATHER NOTES:

NEARBY SIGHTSEEING:

NEARBY RESTAURANTS:

NEARBY GROCERY STORE: ☐ 0-5 MIN.	☐ 5-10 MIN	☐ 10-20 MIN.	☐ 20-30 MIN.	☐ 30+ MIN.

OTHER GROCERY NOTES:

NEARBY PLACES VISITED:

VISIT / DO NEXT TIME:

DESTINATION:	DATES:
TRAVELLED FROM:	TO
VIA	MILEAGE

PREFERRED ROUTES / ROUTES TO AVOID:

SITES ALONG THE WAY:

WEATHER:

CAMPGROUND (NAME, LOCATION, CONTACT, FEES, RESERVATION)

CAMPGROUND PROS AND CONS:

CAMPSITE NUMBER AND DESCRIPTION:

THINGS TO AVOID NEXT TIME:

TRAVELLING COMPANIONS:

THINGS TO REMEMBER FOR NEXT TIME:

RV CAMPGROUND LOGBOOK

LOCAL AREA NOTES				
WEATHER DURING STAY: ☐ VERY COLD	☐ COLD	☐ MODERATE	☐ WARM	☐ HOT

OTHER WEATHER NOTES:

NEARBY SIGHTSEEING:

NEARBY RESTAURANTS:

NEARBY GROCERY STORE: ☐ 0-5 MIN. ☐ 5-10 MIN ☐ 10-20 MIN. ☐ 20-30 MIN. ☐ 30+ MIN.

OTHER GROCERY NOTES:

NEARBY PLACES VISITED:

VISIT / DO NEXT TIME:

DESTINATION:	DATES:
TRAVELLED FROM:	TO
VIA	MILEAGE

PREFERRED ROUTES / ROUTES TO AVOID:

SITES ALONG THE WAY:

WEATHER:

CAMPGROUND (NAME, LOCATION, CONTACT, FEES, RESERVATION)

CAMPGROUND PROS AND CONS:

CAMPSITE NUMBER AND DESCRIPTION:

THINGS TO AVOID NEXT TIME:

TRAVELLING COMPANIONS:

THINGS TO REMEMBER FOR NEXT TIME:

RV PHOTO GALLERY

LOCATION	LOCATION
PHOTO	PHOTO
DATE:	DATE:

LOCATION	LOCATION
PHOTO	PHOTO
DATE:	DATE:

LOCATION	LOCATION
PHOTO	PHOTO
DATE:	DATE:

NOTES

RV PHOTO GALLERY

LOCATION		LOCATION	
PHOTO		PHOTO	
DATE:		DATE:	

LOCATION		LOCATION	
PHOTO		PHOTO	
DATE:		DATE:	

LOCATION		LOCATION	
PHOTO		PHOTO	
DATE:		DATE:	

NOTES

DAILY RV PLANNER

	DESTINATION	ACTIVITIES
DAY 1		
DAY 2		
DAY 3		
DAY 4		
DAY 5		
DAY 6		
DAY 7		

DAILY RV PLANNER

	DESTINATION	ACTIVITIES
DAY 1		
DAY 2		
DAY 3		
DAY 4		
DAY 5		
DAY 6		
DAY 7		

WEEKLY RV SCHEDULE

LOCATION	SUN	MON	TUE	WED	THU	FRI	SAT

REMINDERS	LIST
○	○
○	○
○	○
○	○
○	○
○	○
○	○
○	○
○	○
○	○
○	○
○	○

WEEKLY RV SCHEDULE

LOCATION	SUN	MON	TUE	WED	THU	FRI	SAT

REMINDERS	LIST
○	○
○	○
○	○
○	○
○	○
○	○
○	○
○	○
○	○
○	○
○	○
○	○

INDEX

IDEAS AND NOTES

Name: _____

Made in the USA
Middletown, DE
15 July 2022

69408901R00057